HAND KNITTING

Discover the easiest way to knit!

Larissa Koedyker

Dedication:

This book is dedicated to my family:

My husband, Harvey; my daughters, Yuliya and Krystyna;

my son-in-law, Tyler, and my stepson Tyler.

They encouraged me and helped me to start and run my business.

Special "Thank You" to:

Jim McFarlin – Editor and friend, who supported and inspired my desire to write this book.

Sarah Ebel – My Personal Assistant, for her tremendous help making this book a reality and for being a beautiful model in pictures for this book.

Nick Hirdes (N-Lens Productions) – BeCozi® photographer and videographer, for the beautiful pictures in this book.

Copyright © 2021 by Larissa Koedyker/BeCozi®

All rights reserved. No part of this publication may be reproduced, distributed, or transmitted in any form or by any means, including photocopying, recording, or other electronic or mechanical methods, without the prior written permission of the publisher, except in the case of brief quotations embodied in critical reviews and certain other noncommercial uses permitted by copyright law. For permission requests, write to the author, addressed "Attention: Permissions" at info@becozi.net.

BeCozi®
12950 James St
Holland, MI 49424
www.becozi.com

Ordering Information:
For details, contact: info@becozi.net

Print ISBN: 978-1-63972-017-0

Printed in the United States of America by
Holland Litho Printing Services, Zeeland, MI

First edition

What is the most popular trend in knitting now?
HAND KNITTING!

It is *EASY!*

The easiest way to knit a chunky blanket, rug or a pillow with no special skills!

It's very *FAST!*

The only way to knit something amazing in no time: like a blanket in a few hours.

It is so much *FUN!*

Hand knitting bring so much joy, it calms you down and makes you feel incredibly good.

Contents

Introduction.................................... 7
What Our Customers Say About BeCozi®... 11

Chapter 1: Chunky Yarns
Super Chunky Merino Wool................ 13
Felted Super Chunky Merino Wool....... 13
Super Chunky Vegan Yarn................. 14
Tube Yarn...................................... 14
BeCozi® Chunky Chenille® Yarn.......... 15
Jumbo Chenille Yarn........................ 15
Variegated Chenille Yarn................... 16
Speckled Chenille Yarn..................... 16
Plush Chenille Yarn.......................... 17
Velvet Tube Yarn............................. 17

Chapter 2: Hand Knitting: The Basics
Why Hand Knitting?........................ 19

Chapter 3: Getting Started
How Much Yarn Will You Need?......... 21
Merino Wool and Vegan Yarn............ 21
BeCozi® Chunky Chenille® Yarn......... 21

Jumbo Chenille Yarn........................ 21
Next Steps..................................... 22

Chapter 4: Hand Knit a Merino Wool Blanket................... 24

Chapter 5: Patterns
Round Pillow................................. 37
Seed Stitch................................... 41
Cable Knit Blanket.......................... 47
2x2 Rib Blanket.............................. 54
Chunky Knit Pouf/Ottoman............... 60
Donut Pillow.................................. 65
Twisted Stitch................................ 71
Cat Bed....................................... 77
Knitwear...................................... 84
Hat with a Pom Pom....................... 85
Scarf with Pockets.......................... 93
Useful Techniques.......................... 102
Joining Super Chunky Merino Wool..... 102
Make a Pom Pom........................... 104

Introduction

I was born and raised in Ukraine. I moved to the United States in March of 2005 to marry my husband, Harvey, who lived in Holland, Michigan.

How did a woman from Ukraine meet and fall in love with a man who lives in a small Midwestern town 8,100 miles away, you ask? Why, the internet, of course!

I wanted to meet and marry an American man, as women in Ukraine believe American men make good husbands. I placed my profile on a few dating sites and after a few-year search I met Harvey on the now-defunct Yahoo Personals. (The moral, ladies: never give up hope!) He flew to Ukraine to meet me; we fell in love and nine months later I came to America and became his wife.

We have been happily married since April 2005. Harvey is not just my beloved husband and the father of our children: he is also my partner in the BeCozi® company. In June 2021 he retired from his job at Hope College in Holland, where he had served for almost 20 years, to become our company's full-time CFO. BeCozi® would never be as successful as it has become without his excellent financial knowledge and expertise.

It was a long journey to get to this point, however. After coming to America and working in a few different jobs, I opened an Adoption consulting business in 2010 to help American families to adopt children from Ukraine who were older or had special needs. Ultimately, I helped bring almost 100 children

to the U.S., but in the fall of 2015, I had to close my business due to changes in adoption law and a war in Ukraine.

I started looking for another job or business opportunity when I saw an online video of a British woman who was Arm knitting a huge blanket with super chunky Merino wool in the fall of 2015. I had been a knitter since I was in middle school, when all girls were required to take "Labor classes" and were taught to knit with standard size needles. So, I immediately wanted to try this fun-looking alternative way of knitting.

I started searching for super chunky Merino wool and could find only one company in the U.S. selling it — and at pretty high prices. I bought some Merino wool there anyway and tried my hand, or arm, at "Arm knitting."

I did not like it.

In Arm knitting, the wool is hanging on your arms. The stitches are too big, and I couldn't see what I was knitting while the too-heavy blanket I was making was in my way. So instead, I placed my knitting project in front of me on a coffee table and began using my **hands** as the needles. And that is how Hand knitting was born.

I turned to Google and discovered that Arm knitting is a long-known technique and that there were a few crafty ladies in the U.S. and England who were arm knitting and selling their Merino wool blankets mostly on Etsy back in 2015. Arm knitting became even more popular that year when a girl from Ukraine, Anna, opened a Kickstarter campaign and her videos on Arm knitting with Merino wool exploded all over social media in America. That exposure prompted people to begin looking for Merino wool, but like me, they found it almost impossible to obtain in the U.S.

By that time, I had identified a few Merino wool suppliers outside the country and realized I could sell it in the U.S. for people who would like to try chunky knitting. That's how the idea to launch my own yarn company was born in the fall of 2015.

My older daughter, Yuliya, and her husband Tyler came to visit us for Christmas that year and I proudly announced to all my family my decision to start a company selling Merino wool and hand-knitted blankets. Everybody was extremely supportive and loved the idea. And really, how could anyone not love the idea after touching a super-soft Merino wool blanket? I had made a few of them by that time, along with some scarves and pet beds.

So, my whole family pitched in and started laying the groundwork for actually opening my business during that Christmas holiday. Yuliya created a website and took beautiful pictures of my first creations, as she happens to be a professional photographer who is also very familiar with creating websites. Yuliya was our devoted photographer for 4 years making beautiful pictures for BeCozi®.

Our younger daughter, Krystyna, became our first model. Our cats and a dog, Walle, became our pet models. And Tyler is the one who came up with the name of our company. He initially suggested Be Cozy: after some creative thinking, we ended up with "BeCozi®." It was a very memorable time and I am forever thankful to my family for their help in creating BeCozi®!

I loved my newly invented way of Hand knitting with super chunky Merino wool so much, I decided to share my passion with others. With the encouragement of my friend, Nancy, in May 2016 I created a BeCozi® YouTube channel, youtube.com/c/becozi, and started posting my videos showing people how they, too, could Hand knit blankets, scarves and other chunky items.

BeCozi® started as a hobby. For the first year and a half we operated our small business from our home. However, the business kept expanding as we added new yarns to our stock, so in the summer of 2017 we rented a small office.

Within the next two years we expanded to the three other offices in the same building, but by 2019 we realized we still needed a bigger space. We started looking to rent or purchase a larger facility but could not find anything that would accommodate our growing business.

After some consideration we decided to build our own building.

On May 13, 2019 we made an offer for a piece of land that had been for sale for 10 years. Of course, as fate would have it, the same day we made our offer we received a call from our realtor telling us another company had just made an offer, too! We countered with a little bit more money and won the bid!

We started working on our architectural plans and bank loan. Four months later, on October 22, the construction phase of our new building began.

We used a great local construction company, Miedema Construction from Hudsonville, Mich. Just five short months later, our building was ready to move into! Unfortunately, however, the State of Michigan announced its first COVID lockdown on March 23, 2020 and we had to wait to move in into our brand-new building until May 12.

Today we are operating BeCozi® from our new facility, custom built for our needs, and enjoying every moment of running our own business from our own building!

As our business has grown, we've added a few more chunky yarns to our online store, **becozi.com**: today, BeCozi® is the biggest supplier of chunky yarns in America. We sell BeCozi Chunky Chenille® and Jumbo chenille yarn, super chunky Merino wool, felted Merino wool, super chunky Vegan yarn, Tube and "Plush and Lush" Velvet yarn, "Forever Soft" Merino, "Furreal Soft" and Chunky Loopy stitch yarn.

Our felted Merino wool is a custom-made wool: using our "know-how" technique, a super chunky Merino wool is being felted to become stronger and more durable. BeCozi Chunky Chenille® yarn was discovered and began to be sold by BeCozi® in the spring of 2016; now it is being sold in many big craft stores under different names. Jumbo chenille yarn is our custom-created yarn, available only at **becozi.com**. There is also our "Plush and Lush" Velvet yarn — custom made, super chunky and created according to our exact specifications.

We are thinking about adding more chunky yarns, as craft stores typically do not carry them (except for Chunky Chenille yarn), because Hand knitting with chunky yarns is on the rise!

The BeCozi® business grew significantly during the coronavirus pandemic. People were stuck at home and needed something to do: Hand knitting and chunky knitting with big needles was that "something" that helped people to stay sane during long periods of isolation.

Some people questioned the Hand knitting technique as my invention, arguing that it was known long before I started my business and my YouTube channel. If you're looking for a definition of Hand knitting, it is a form of knitting in which the knitted item is produced by hands using needles. It's the opposite of machine knitting, where a machine is used for knitting something.

Back in 2015 when I created my Hand knitting technique — knitting with super chunky Merino wool and using only hands, not arms, instead of needles — this method was not known. I searched all over the internet and YouTube: there was *nobody* on YouTube who was demonstrating how to do it, and you could still not find a definition on Google of Hand knitting in the way I created it.

Finger knitting has been known for a long time but this technique has been used for knitting with thin yarns using your fingers, not hands.

This is the reason I am writing this book: to share the Hand knitting technique with big, chunky yarns that was created by me in 2015, and to share some of my most popular Hand knitting projects.

As of fall 2023, BeCozi® has posted more than 225 videos on their YouTube showing our Hand knitting technique. We have 156,000 YouTube subscribers and more than 16 million views to date.

BeCozi® videos have been copied many times by people all over the world. You can find hundreds of videos showing Hand knitting styles with chunky yarns on YouTube now (with no credit to BeCozi®). Hundreds of people decided to show how to Hand knit on YouTube and other social media outlets, with new videos popping up all the time. Many of them are doing it just for fun, but some have actually created businesses copying our videos.

Fact: BeCozi® is the only YouTuber that created the Hand knitting style and began showing "how-to" videos in May 2016. We now have more than 225 videos, and we post new video tutorials on a regular basis teaching people how to Hand knit.

After BeCozi® posted its first videos in 2016, teaching how to Hand knit blankets with BeCozi super chunky Merino wool, a massive new wave of Hand knitting exploded all across America. Many art studios and individuals with entrepreneurial visions started offering Hand knitting classes, teaching people how to Hand knit blankets with chunky yarns, mostly BeCozi Chunky Chenille® and/or its copies.

Because Hand knitting has become so very popular now, I decided to write this book. It is my greatest desire to introduce Hand knitting to everybody who would like to learn this very fun and easy way to express your creativity!

What Our Customers Say About BeCozi®

" It is great dealing with a company that cares and does not hesitate to communicate and please their customers. "

– Denise

" After losing both of my hands due to illness, I am so thankful to Larissa for opening up my world again to being able to create things. I hope anyone who hesitates to do this will give it a try. It really is possible. "

– Linda

" I am 64 years old. I have always liked to crochet. I tried to learn to knit, but couldn't master the needles. When I discovered Larissa's videos, I was so excited! I finally could knit! "

– Patsy

" Knitting these chunky blankets for my family and good friends has become my new crafting passion. I get so much joy in ordering the yarn and knitting up these beautiful blankets for all of the very special people in my life. "

– Jeannette

" I love my new hobby! "

– Anne-Marie

" I have Parkinson's disease, which has affected my right side. Hand knitting has helped me to relax and focus. It has improved the dexterity of my right hand and lessened my tremors while knitting. I've also become very productive, which is a great mental boost. "

– Linda

" I have learned to make these blankets and pillows from Larissa's tutorial videos and have been so blessed by them! Thank you so much for your items, videos, and inspiration! "

– Karen

" I discovered your wonderful videos when we shut down because of COVID. I was working from home for 3 and 1/2 months and wanted a new, easy hobby. Since then I have made several things. Thank you so much for all your wonderful videos. They make it so easy. "

– Melanie

Chapter 1: Chunky Yarns

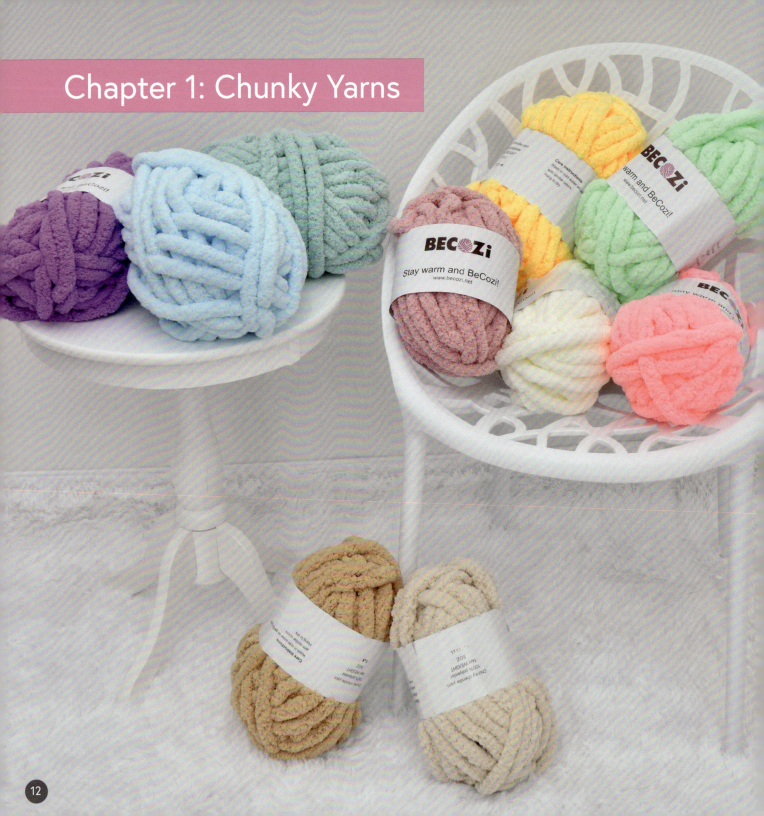

Here we will introduce some chunky yarn we are using for Hand knitting projects

Super Chunky Merino Wool

It is 100% pure Australian Merino sheep wool. Super soft, gentle to the touch, hypoallergenic, moisture wicking. This super thick yarn is also called "roving." It is great for Hand and Arm knitting of blankets for decorative purposes. This fiber is very gentle and not recommended for creating products for everyday use. *Care: dry cleaning is recommended.*

Felted Super Chunky Merino Wool

The same 100% pure Australian Merino wool that was felted in a special way to prevent any shedding or pilling. Felted Merino wool is thinner and stiffer than the non-felted variety but it is very strong and durable. It is good for Hand and Arm knitting blankets, rugs, pillows and other products for frequent use. *Care: can be washed on a gentle quick cycle. Hang to dry.*

Super Chunky Vegan Yarn

This yarn is an alternative to Merino wool: it is super soft and gentle to touch, looks and feels like Merino wool but it is 100% Acrylic. It is good for Hand and Arm knitting of blankets, pillows, sweaters, scarves, hats and anything else. Blankets made with vegan yarn are good for decorative purposes.
Care: Dry cleaning.

Tube Yarn

This yarn is a cotton tube filled with polyester stuffing. It is bulky but stretchy and great for Hand and Arm knitting of big, heavy blankets, rugs, pillows, pet beds, baby beds, and many other products.
Care: can be washed in cold or warm water and dried in a dryer on medium heat.

BeCozi® Chunky Chenille® Yarn

We discovered this yarn in February 2016 when it was not known to a knitting market. This super soft and beautiful yarn is 100% polyester. It is perfect for Hand or Arm knitting or knitting with big needles. Anything can be knitted with this yarn: a soft blanket that can be used on an everyday basis; a rug, pillow, sweater, hat, scarf, baby nest, cat bed, cardigan, or anything you can dream of — the possibilities are endless! *Care: wash in a cold water on gentle/quick cycle. Dry in a dryer on a low/medium heat.*

Jumbo Chenille Yarn

This yarn is one of a kind: it was custom made for BeCozi® and there is nothing like it on the market today: only at becozi.com. It is super thick chenille yarn, about 1 1/4-inch thick (BeCozi® Chunky Chenille® is about 2/3 of an inch thick). Jumbo chenille yarn is super soft and fluffy: touching it is like touching a cloud. It is perfect for Hand or Arm knitting that super soft blanket, pillow or baby blanket to enjoy its softness. *Care: can be washed on a gentle/quick cycle; hang to dry or dry in a dryer on low/medium heat.*

Variegated Chenille Yarn

This beautiful chunky chenille yarn has been created by our company to bring some bright colors for Hand knitting with chenille yarn! It has all properties of Chunky chenille yarn. This yarn can be used for any chunky knitting project: blanket, rug, scarf or a hat. *Care: wash in cold/warm water on quick cycle, dry in a dryer or low/medium heat.*

Tie-Dye Chenille Yarn

Newest addition — custom made Chenille yarn dyed in a special tie-dye method, a very unique and new to the Chenille yarn market.
Care: wash in cold/warm water; dry in a dryer on low/medium heat.

Plush Chenille Yarn

This yarn is another recent addition to the chunky yarn collection: it is 50% Acrylic and 50% Polyester (chunky and jumbo chenille yarns are 100% Acrylic). This combination makes it plushy with the look and feel of velvet fabric. It is also super soft and perfect for chunky knitting. It is used for chunky knitting, the same as Chunky chenille yarn. *Care: wash in cold/warm water; dry in a dryer on low/medium heat.*

Velvet Tube Yarn

Velvet tube yarn made with velvet fabric and filled with polyester stuffing. It is super soft and beautiful and it is great for making super bulky plush blankets and pillows! *Care: wash on cold/warm cycle, dry in a dryer on low or medium heat.*

Chapter 2: Hand Knitting: The Basics

Why Hand Knitting?

If you have ever tried the regular way of knitting with needles, liked it or not, succeeded or not, or even if you have never tried knitting at all — Hand knitting is by far the simplest and easiest way of knitting and can be done by anybody!

It does not require special skills and it is very therapeutic. We have so many followers and customers who started Hand knitting for dealing with medical issues such as anxiety, depression, and even cancer! Among the recent stories: Hand knitting has been shown to be very helpful to Parkinson's disease patients. It improves their health both mentally and physically.

Hand knitting was created for knitting with big, super chunky yarn like super chunky Merino wool, which is about 2 1/2-3 inches thick. Hand knitting with Merino wool is extremely fast — you can make a large blanket in 45-60 minutes with no practice at all! Some practice would be good, however, as it will give your stitches a more even look.

Hand knitting is very unique because you are knitting a project back and forth (left to right, right to left) unlike knitting with needles when you need to turn the project to the back every other row. Another unique feature of Hand knitting is that you can cast off (finish) the project from either left or right side.

Nowadays the Hand knitting technique is used mostly for knitting blankets with Chunky Chenille yarn and its other different names and also different chunky acrylic and polyester yarns. Super chunky Merino wool is still in big demand, though, as nothing looks as good as a blanket Hand knitted with super thick and soft Merino wool. Just remember — a Merino wool blanket is like your grandmother's China tea set — it is good for decoration purposes. If used on a daily basis, it can still be soft and warm but it will lose its beautiful look.

For Hand knitting you need only your hands and a space where you can place any chunky yarn: a table, a bed or even some space on a floor. We Hand knit all our products on custom made wooden tables. I created a design for a Hand knitting table and it is a very comfortable for Hand knitting. Our company, BeCozi®, is considering creating portable, foldable Hand knitting tables for sale that everyone who like Hand knitting could use in their home! In this book we will be showing you some Hand knitting techniques with super chunky Merino wool and also patterns for BeCozi® Chunky Chenille® yarn and Jumbo chenille yarn.

So, let's get started!

Chapter 3: Getting Started

How Much Yarn Will You Need?

We will give you an estimated amount for a small, medium, large and extra-large size blanket to Hand knit with BeCozi® most popular yarns. You can substitute most of these yarn with other chunky yarns available at the market now.

Merino wool (about 2.5 in thick) and Vegan yarn (about 2 in thick):

- Small lap throw, 30x50 inches — 4 lbs.; this size is a small throw to cover your legs while sitting on a couch; start with 12 stitches

- Medium size blanket, 40x60 inches — 7 lbs.; enough to cover a medium-sized person from toes to neck (cover, not curl up in); start with 16 stitches

- Large size blanket, 50x70 inches — 10 lbs.; this blanket will cover most of a Queen size bed; start with 20 stitches

- Extra Large size blanket, 60x80 inches — 14 lbs.; this blanket will cover a Queen size bed from edge to edge; start with 24 stitches

How to calculate the amount of Merino wool needed:

- Multiply the width of the blanket you're making by its length and divide by 350

BeCozi® Chunky Chenille® Yarn (or any other chunky chenille yarn):

- Small lap throw, 30x50 inches — 5 skeins; this size is a small throw to cover your legs while sitting on a couch; start with 19 stitches

- Medium size blanket, 40x60 inches — 7 skeins; enough to cover a medium size person from toes to neck (cover, not curl up in); start with 24 stitches

- Large size blanket, 50x70 inches — 10 skeins; this blanket will cover most of a Queen size bed; start with 29 stitches

- Extra Large size blanket, 60x80 inches — 14 skeins; this blanket will cover a Queen size bed from edge to edge; start with 34 stitches

Jumbo Chenille Yarn (about 1 1/3 of an inch thick):

- Small lap throw, 30x50 inches — 6 skeins; this size is a small throw to cover your legs while sitting on a couch; start with 14 stitches

- Medium size blanket, 40x60 inches — 9 skeins; enough to cover a medium size person from toes to neck (cover, not curl up in); start with 18 stitches

- Large size blanket, 50x70 inches — 12 skeins; this blanket will cover most of a Queen size bed; start with 23 stitches

- Extra Large size blanket, 60x80 inches — 17 skeins; this blanket will cover a Queen size bed from edge to edge; start with 28 stitches

Calculate the amount of Jumbo chenille needed (not applicable to other chunky chenille yarn):

- Multiply the width of a blanket you wish to make by its length, then divide by 250

Calculate the amount of BeCozi® tube/velvet yarn needed (not applicable to other tube/velvet yarn):

- Multiple the width of a blanket you wish to make by its length, then divide by 215

Next steps

Find a place where you will be Hand knitting. The easiest place to do it: on a kitchen table. Our custom-made Hand knitting table is made tilted: the side farthest from you is higher than the front edge. This way it is much easier to Hand knit. To have the same comfortable place for knitting, try placing something under the far legs of your table, lifting it a bit to make your knitting process easier.

Calculate the number of stitches you will need for your knitted project. We will give you some measurements for our most popular products:

- Merino wool blanket: divide the width of the blanket by 2.5 — get the number of stitches to start

- Chunky Chenille yarn: divide the width of the blanket by 1.63

- Jumbo chenille yarn: divide the width of the blanket by 2.2

- Velvet yarn: divide the width of the blanket by 2.2

- Tube yarn: divide the width of the blanket by 2.8

Now, when you have the yarn in the right amount and a place for Hand knitting...

Let's get started!

Note: always make a simple knot on both ends of chenille yarn; cut the tail close to the knot: it prevents the yarn from unraveling when it is used/washed. Same for Jumbo chenille.

Chapter 4: Hand Knit a Merino Wool Blanket

Cast on: Place the yarn in front of you this way.

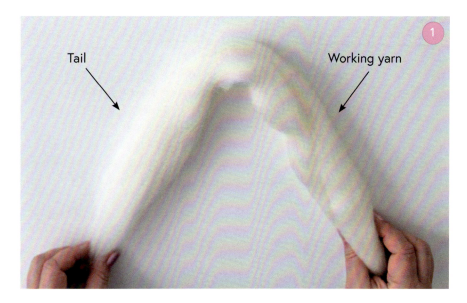

Tail / Working yarn

Make a loop.

Insert your hand inside the loop.

Grab working yarn and pull it out.

Your first stitch is ready.

Now we will be "casting on": making a chain of the stitches as the first one.

Insert your hand into the first stitch.

Grab working yarn and pull it through.

Keep casting on using the same technique until you have the number of stitches required for your project: insert your hand inside the stitch, grab working yarn.

Pull it out.

When a chain of stitches is cast on, turn it on the other side.

> *We do it this way because we want to make sure the bottom of the blanket will have a chain and look beautiful and well made.*

1st Row: We will be using the middle part of every stitch for knitting our first row: I am pointing to it in the picture.

We will be skipping the first stitch to make the right side border look nice.

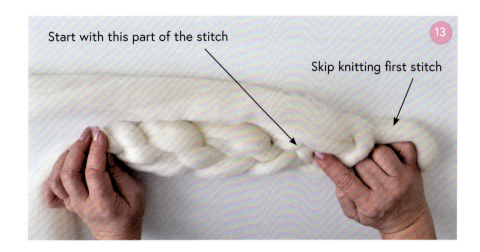

We are now starting to knit/pull out our first row.

Insert your right hand into the stitch.

Grab working yarn and pull it through.

You pulled out your second stitch (we skipped the first).

Repeat the same technique with your third stitch and all the other stitches in the row.

You are done with your first row!

2nd Row: Using the same technique we used for the first row: insert your hand inside the first stitch, grab working yarn.

Pull it through.

Make second stitch the same way: insert your hand inside.

Grab working yarn, pull it out. Keep knitting this way to the end of the row.

You have now Hand knitted two rows!

3rd Row: Starting with this row, we will NOT be knitting the FIRST stitch in every row. We will start with knitting the SECOND stitch.

Why are we doing it this way? When you skip the FIRST stitch in every row, you create a beautiful chain on both sides of your blanket. The sides will not be curling, they will remain straight and look professionally made. Also, you will use less yarn, which is quite important when using Merino wool because it is pricey.

Please, look at the picture above: you simply place the first stitch to the side and start knitting the new row with the second stitch.

Keep Hand knitting all the stitches in 3rd row the same way we did in the previous row: Insert your hand inside, grab working yarn, pull it out. When knitting from **left** to right — we use our **left** hand to knit; when knitting from **right** to left: we use our **right** hand.

Make sure to KNIT the LAST stitch in every row. *SKIP the FIRST stitch, KNIT the LAST stitch.*

Now when we have our first three rows knitted, the rest will be easy: just keep Hand knitting all the rows in the same way back and forth!

Hint: to count rows, count chains.

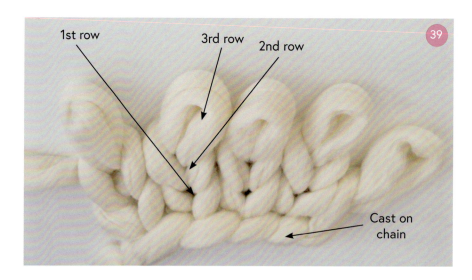

If you are using a table for Hand knitting, after about 5-10 rows depending on the yarn you use, your blanket will become longer and start falling off the table.

To avoid this: roll the end of the blanket in front of you up to the row you are knitting and keep rolling it as it becomes longer — this way it will be rolled in front of you and won't be falling off the table.

When you reach the desired length of your blanket, you will need to have a certain length amount of yarn left: three widths of a blanket. **Now it is time to cast off**.

Insert your hand into the first two stitches.

Grab working yarn and pull it through both stitches.

You now have one stitch made from two!

Repeat the same technique for the next two stitches.

You made another stitch from two.

Keep casting off this way (knitting two stitches at a time) until you have one stitch left.

Now you need to insert the tail inside the last stitch and pull it until the stitch is closed.

Pull gently on the tail to keep it from breaking!

Now we will weave in (hide) those ends of the yarn on the back of the knitting:

Turn the blanket on the back side.

Find the stitch to hide the end.

Insert the end in that stitch.

Repeat to hide the end completely.

Like this.

For Merino wool, here's another way to do it — use a felting needle and a felting mat to felt the end under one of the stitches on the back of the blanket. (*See Useful Techniques for instructions.*)

Congratulations — you just made your first Hand-knitted blanket!

*Note: Chunky knit blankets are usually used as **accent blankets**, not as comforters. They are usually placed on a footage area of a bed or as a throw on a couch.*

Round Pillow

Level: Beginner

This cute round Merino wool pillow will be your easiest Hand knitting project ever! You can finish it in, literally, 15 to 20 minutes!

What you will need:

- 1 lb of Super Chunky Merino Wool

Cast on 11 stitches: refer to pages 25-26 showing how to cast on (to start).

Connect the chain into a circle by inserting the last stitch into the bottom of first stitch.

1st Row: Knitting in a circle.

Knit six rows around the circle by inserting your hand into the top part of the stitch and pulling the working yarn out as shown in the pictures.

After a few rows, fold the pillow like this and keep knitting for 6 rows.

Now we will connect the bottom of the pillow.

Place the pillow like this:

Insert the tail inside every stitch from inside out.

After inserting the tail in all stitches around, insert the tail into the two stitches that had working yarn in them already.

Gently pull the tail to close the opening.

Push the tail into the center of the pillow so it is hidden.

Turn pillow on another side, leave the tail there.

Place a pillow insert or some stuffing inside the pillow.

Leave a tail at least 10 inches long, break/cut the yarn.

Now we will close the top of the pillow the same way as the bottom.

Insert the tail into every stitch to the left from the inside out.

Continue this all the way around.

Gently pull the yarn to close the opening.

Insert the tail into the two stitches that had working yarn inserted already.

Insert working yarn into the middle of the pillow.

Your beautiful round Merino wool pillow is ready!

Seed Stitch

Level: Intermediate

Seed stitch looks very beautiful on Merino wool blanket. Stitches are big and chunky. This pattern is popular for other chunky yarns also.

Project: Small Blanket 30" x 50"

What you will need:

4 lbs. of super chunky Merino wool, mustard color; felting mat and needle (optional).

Start with casting on:

- 12 stitches for Merino wool and tube yarn;
- 14 stitches for felted Merino wool and velvet yarn, vegan yarn and jumbo chenille
- 19 stitches for Chunky chenille yarn

(Refer to Chapter 1 for information about number of stitches.)

Cast on 12 stitches: (refer to pages 25-26 to learn how).

1st Row: Turn the chain over so the bottom of the chain is showing.

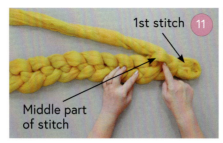

Middle part of stitch — 1st stitch

Keep the first stitch out and start pulling out stitches for the 1st row using the middle part of every stitch.

Insert your hand into the middle part of the second stitch. Grab working yarn.

Pull working yarn out to make your second stitch.

Repeat these steps until you reach the end of the row.

2nd Row: Start the Seed pattern.

Knit the first stitch by inserting your hand inside the first stitch.

Grab working yarn.

Pull the yarn out.

Place working yarn on top of the next stitch.

Grab the stitch with you left hand and working yarn with your right one.

Push working yarn through the stitch to the back.

Pull the stitch up from the back.

Continue the pattern — knit one stitch, purl next stitch — to the end of the row.

Knit one stitch.

Purl the next one.

This is how your pattern will look with 2 rows knitted (first row pulled out, second row — started Seed stitch pattern).

3rd Row: alternate stitches.

Knit the stitches that were purled.

Purl the stitches that were knitted.

Keep knitting stitches this way to the end of the row.

4th Row: alternate stitches again: *In every row you will knit the stitches that were purled, purl the stitches that were knitted.*

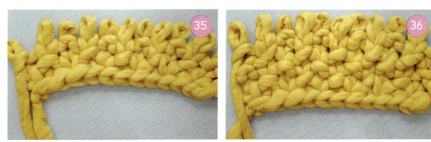

Knit until you have the yarn left enough to cast off the blanket: three widths of the blanket.

Casting off: (refer to pages 31-32 to see how)

Continue casting off until you have one stitch left.

Break the yarn and insert the tail into the stitch.

Gently pull through the stitch to make a knot.

Weave in the tail to hide it.

Your Seed stitch blanket is ready!

Cable Knit Blanket

Level: Intermediate

The cable knit pattern is an all-time favorite! Those cables look so beautiful with Chunky Chenille yarn.

What you need for a medium size blanket 40x60 inches:

- Seven skeins of Chunky Chenille yarn
- Scissors

Cast on 21 stitches: refer to pages 25-26 to learn how.

Turn the chain over.

1st Row: Pull up the stitches using the middle part of the stitch.

Skip the first stitch.

Insert your hand inside the middle part of second stitch, grab working yarn and pull it out.

Repeat to all stitches to pull out first row.

2nd Row: Starting Cable knit pattern.

Knit 1, Purl 2, Knit 3, Purl 3 Knit 3, Purl 3, Knit 3, Purl 2, Knit 1

Knit 1 stitch:

Insert your hand into the stitch, grab working yarn and pull it out through the stitch.

Purl 2 stitches:

Place working yarn on top of the next stitch and push working yarn through the stitch from front to back.

Knit 3 stitches.

Purl 3 stitches.

Knit 3 stitches.

Purl 3 stitches, Knit 3 stitches.

Purl 2 stitches.

Knit the last stitch.

3rd Row: Follow the pattern (Read the pattern from right to left).

Knit 1, Purl 2, Knit 3, Purl 3, Knit 3, Purl 3, Knit 3, Purl 2, Knit 1

Knit 1 stitch.

Purl 2 stitches.

Knit 3 stitches.

Purl 3 stitches.

Knit 3 stitches.

Continue the pattern:

Purl 3, Knit 3, Purl 2, Knit 1 to the end of the row.

4th Row: Continue this pattern.

5th-6th Rows: Continue the pattern for 6 rows total.

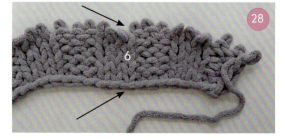

7th Row: Start the cable twist on knitted stitches in this row.

To make the twist: Cross the stitch on the right (#3) under the two stitches on the left (#1 and #2).

Like this.

Knit the twist: Knit the two stitches that are crossed over on top.

Knit the stitch that is crossed under.

You've made the first cable twist of the blanket!

Purl the next 3 stitches.

You will now make the middle cable:

Cross the stitch on the right under the 2 stitches on the left.

Knit the 2 stitches first and then the stitch on the back.

Purl the next 3 stitches.

3rd Cable: Cross the stitch on the right under the 2 stitches on the left.

Purl the next 2 stitches, knit the last stitch.

8th Row: After the row with the twists, knit 6 rows following the pattern, then do the cable twists again in 7th row to make the cables.

Knit according to the pattern until you have a tail that is equal to three lengths of the blanket.

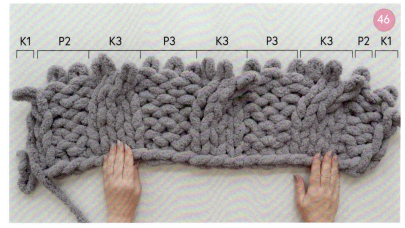

Cast off to finish — refer to pages 31-32.

Your blanket is ready!

2x2 Rib Blanket

Level: Intermediate

This blanket is made using Jumbo chenille yarn.

Size 30x50 inches — a small lap throw, enough to cover your legs while sitting on a couch.

What you need for a 30x50 blanket:

- Six Skeins of Jumbo Chenille yarn (3 skeins of gray color, 3 skeins of ivory)
- Scissors

Cast on 12 stitches (refer to pages 25-26 to see how).

1st Row: Turn the chain over.

Skip the first stitch.

Insert your hand into the middle of the next stitch.

Grab working yarn.

Pull it out to make a stitch.

Insert your hand into the middle of the next stitch.

Grab working yarn and pull the yarn out.

Repeat these steps until you've pulled stitches to the end of the row.

2nd Row: Insert your hand into the first stitch.

Grab working yarn and pull it out.

You just knitted the first stitch.

Knit the next stitch.

Purl the next 2 stitches:

Place working yarn on top of the next stitch.

Push working yarn through the loop to the back and pull the stitch out.

Purl second stitch.

Knit the next 2 stitches:

Purl the next 2 stitches.

Continue this way (Knit 2 stitches, Purl 2 stitches) until the end of the row.

Repeat this pattern until you use all of your first color.

We will now be adding the second color.

Join the colors by tying them into a knot. Make the knot very tight. Cut the tails close to the knot.

Continue the pattern with the new color.

(Knit 2 stitches, Purl 2 stitches)

Switch to another color when the current color is used by making a simple knot.

The new color should always start at the beginning of a row. **If you don't have enough yarn to start a new color with a new row**, unwind the yarn to the previous row, connect the new color and cut the yarn: you can use it later.

After repeating your colors to the desired length of the blanket, cast off and weave in the tail to finish!

Note: You will need some yarn left to cast off: three widths of the blanket (**Cast off:** pages 31-32).

Cast off by knitting two stitches at a time.

Until you have one left.

Insert tail inside last stitch, pull it.

Weave it in on the back of the blanket.

The blanket is ready!

Chunky Knit Pouf/Ottoman

Level: Beginner

This pouf is pretty easy to make and will be a great addition to any room in your house.

What you need:

- 4 lbs of tube yarn
- A pouf insert (You can use a few pillows)
- Scissors
- Needle and thread

Cast on 16 stitches (refer to pages 25-26 to see how).

Connect the chain to make a circle by inserting the tail into the base of the last stitch on the right.

1st Row: Knit in the circle by pulling out every stitch on the left through the back part of each stitch on a chain.

Use the back part of the stitch.

Insert your hand inside the first stitch on the left from the connection point.

Grab working yarn and pull it out to make a stitch.

Keep knitting all stitches around the circle.

2nd-10th Row: Continue knitting in the circle for 10 more rows (11 rows total).

When you have 3 rows knitted — fold your project in half, as shown in the picture 17, and keep knitting until you have 11 rows.

Now we will be closing the bottom opening of the pouf.

Place the pouf bottom up.

Insert the tail into each stitch of the bottom chain.

(Be sure to insert the tail from the inside out to give it a clean look.)

Now pull the tail to close up the hole. Then insert the tail to the inside of the pouf and weave it into a stitch on the inside to secure it. Turn in on another side.

If you want to be sure it won't come undone, you can sew the tail to a stitch.

Take the insert and put it into the project. *(You may need to wiggle it around to get it to sit inside the knitted cover comfortably).*

Connect the top of the pouf: insert the tail into each stitch around, from the inside out. *(Be sure to keep the first stitch from unraveling).*

 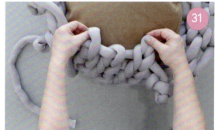

Pull tightly to close the top of the pouf.

Insert the tail into the next few stitches to keep it snug. Then insert the tail into the center of the closing to hide it.

Your pouf is done!

Donut Pillow

Level: Intermediate

This cute pillow looks very cute when it is knitted with big, chunky yarn: we will make it with our Jumbo chenille yarn. Another option — Super Chunky Merino wool.

Care: Jumbo chenille — can be washed in a washing machine.

Merino wool — dry clean.

What you need:

- 1 skein of Jumbo chenille or 1 lbs of Merino wool
- Stuffing
- Scissors or Felting Mat and Needle for Merino wool (optional)

Cast on 11 stitches (refer to pages 25-26 to see how).

Place the chain into a circle.

Take a tail and insert it into the base of this stitch.

Pull the tail through — you connected the Circle.

1st Row: Knit all stitches in a circle.

Insert your hand into the back side of the first stitch on the left.

Grab working yarn. Pull it through.

Repeat knitting all stitches in a circle.

2nd Row: Knit all stitches around the circle.

By inserting your hand inside the back of every stitch.

Grabbing working yarn and pulling it out.

Keep knitting around this way.

The tail shows you the beginning of the circle.

After knitting a few rows, fold the pillow like in Pictures 18-19.

And keep knitting around turning the pillow back and forth.

To add new skein: make a simple knot.

Pull it gently to make the tight knot.

Cut the tails on both sides of knot, close to it.

This is how the connection will look like.

Knit 10 rows.

Fold the Pillow this way: the bottom in the middle; bottom and top of the Pillow will be side by side.

Cast off: We will need to have some yarn left to finish the Pillow: two widths of the Pillow.

Add some stuffing in the space between the bottom and top.

Insert your hand inside the first stitch on the left (top) AND add the stitch across from the bottom.

Insert working yarn inside two stitches you have on your hand.

You connected first two stitches, top and bottom, and a working yarn is in your left hand.

Repeat: insert your hand inside the next stitch on the top and on the bottom.

Insert working yarn inside both stitches — connect them.

Pull working yarn through the two stitches you just made to make them closer to each other.

Keep connecting top and bottom stitches this way until you connect them all.

Pull working yarn through all stitches to make the opening smaller.

Insert the tail inside two first stitches where you inserted the tail before.

Attach working yarn to any stitch inside by making a knot.

Cut the remaining working yarn or weave it in inside the stitches.

Your donut pillow is ready!

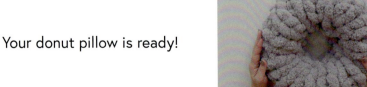

Twisted Stitch

Level: Intermediate

This pattern is one of everybody's favorite. If you Hand knitted a simple stitch blanket — you can easily Hand knit this pattern too. We would not recommend to Hand knit this one as a first-time experience.

What you need for 30x50 blanket:

- 5 skeins of Chunky chenille yarn
- Scissors

Cast on 19 stitches (Refer to pages 25-26 to see how).

1st Row: Turn the chain over; we will use this middle part of every stitch to pull out the first row.

Leave the first stitch laying like this.

Start pulling stitches out with the second stitch:

insert your hand in the middle of the stitch;

grab working yarn, pull it out.

Repeat: pull out all stitches on the chain this way.

We pulled out our first row.

2nd Row: Knit by twisting the stitches from left to right with left side of the stitch going over right.

Twist the first stitch.

See this twist on the bottom of the stitch.

Now knit it:

Insert your hand inside the twisted stitch, grab working yarn, pull it out. First twisted stitch in the 1st row is ready.

Twist the second stitch the same way, from left to right: left side of the stitch going over right.

Insert your hand inside the twisted stitch, grab working yarn.

Pull it out.

Keep twisting all stitches from left to right till the end of the 1st row.

The 1st row will look like this.

2nd Row: *Twisting stitches from right to left: right side of the stitch goes over left.*

Twist the first stitch.

  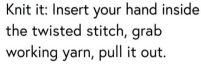

Knit it: Insert your hand inside the twisted stitch, grab working yarn, pull it out.

Twist every stitch in 2nd row the same way: right side goes over left and then knit it.

Repeat to the end of the row.

3rd Row: repeat 1st row — twist all stitches from left to right.

Twist all stitches from left to right till the end of the row.

3rd row is done!

4th Row: (to the end of the blanket): repeat rows 1-2.

Casting off: Keep a tail of working yarn in the length of three widths of the blanket.

Cast off by knitting two stitches at a time until you have one left:
(refer to pages 31-32 for details)

  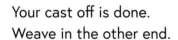

Insert working yarn into the last stitch.

Pull it, weave in the tail.

Your cast off is done. Weave in the other end.

Your blanket is ready!

Cat Bed

Level: Beginner

This cat bed is made with Super chunky Merino wool. It is pretty easy to make, can be done by a beginner.

Care: Can be hand washed in a sink; lay flat to dry.

What you need:

- 1.5 lbs of Super chunky Merino wool
- Scissors
- Felting Mat and Needles for finishing (optional)

Cast on 15 stitches (refer to pages 25-26)

Let's connect the chain into a circle.

Take the tail.

Insert the tail into the base of the last stitch on right.

Pull it through.

You now connected the chain into the circle.

Let's pull out the first row now.

Insert your hand inside this stitch.

Grab working yarn, pull it out.

Do the same with the second stitch.

Pull out all stitches in the first row the same way.

Continue knitting around for 5 more rows. There should be 6 rows total.

After knitting 3 rows, fold the knitting project in two parts. Keep knitting to have 6 rows total.

Now we are going to close the bottom of the bed: Place the bottom of the cat bed in front of you like this.

To close the bottom of the cat bed: insert the tail into each of the bottom chain stitches.

The tail should be inserted from inside out in every stitch.

Gently pull the tail after inserting in every stitch to connect the opening.

Continue all around to the opening until you have the tail inserted in all stitches.

Once the tail is inserted into all bottom stitches, gently pull the tail to close up the bottom.

Now insert the tail inside two stitches on the left that we inserted the tail before.

Insert the tail in the middle of the bed.

Turn the bed on another side and weave in (hide) the tail in between the stitches.

This is the inside of the bed.

We will now **cast off** the top stitches of the cat bed.

Insert your hand into the last stitch and a stitch on the left from it.

Grab working yarn and pull it up through both stitches.

With the stitch still on your hand, add the next stitch to your hand.

Grab working yarn and pull the working yarn to make one stitch from two.

Repeat these steps until you have one stitch left. Make stitches LOOSE otherwise the opening will be too tight.

With your right hand inside the last stitch, insert it into the last stitch on left.

Grab working yarn and pull it out.

This is your last stitch.

Break the wool.

With your hand inside the last stitch, insert it in middle of the first stitch on left.

Grab working yarn and pull it out.

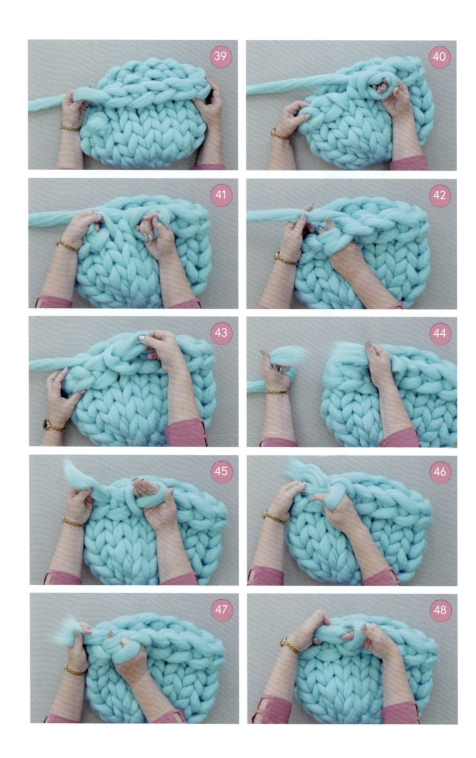

Place the tail inside the stitch on left and weave in the end between stitches inside the bed.

Your cat bed is done!

Knitwear

Hat with a Pom Pom

Level: Beginner

This hat is very easy to Hand knit, even if you have never knitted anything in your life. Make it for yourself or your loved one this season, it will be a hit!

Care: Wash in cold water, gentle cycle, hang to dry.

What you need:

- 0.5 skein (4 oz.) of chunky chenille yarn
- Scissors
- Needle and thread
- Pom Pom

You can make a super chunky Merino wool hat using the same simple technique; start with 11 stitches.

Cast on 13 stitches.
(refer to pages 25-26 to see how).

Connect the yarn into a circle by inserting the tail into the base of the first stitch on the chain.

1st Row: Hand knitting in a circle.

Pull out a stitch through the back of each stitch around the circle.

Insert your hand, grab working yarn, pull it out.

Keep pulling out the stitches all the way around the circle.

Continue to knit around the circle.

When you have 3 rows knitted, fold the project in half and place it flat on the table.

Continue knitting around until you have 7 rows knitted.

Cast off the bottom of the hat: Insert your hand into the last stitch and into the next stitch to the left.

Grab working yarn and pull it through both stitches.

You now have one stitch made from two.

Add a stitch from the left to the one you just made.

Grab working yarn, pull it through both stitches; Continue casting off until you get to the stitch you started with.

We will now insert our hand into the opening in between stitches; grab working yarn, pull it out.

Now you have two stitches on your hand.

Knit them to make one.

With the last stitch on your hand, insert it inside the last stitch on the left.

Grab working yarn, pull it out to make second stitch.

Push a stitch on left through the stitch on right:

You now have one stitch.

Now, with a stitch on your right hand, insert your hand in the middle of the stitch on left; pull the tail through two stitches.

Insert the tail inside the next stitch.

Weave the tail in (hide) in between the stitches inside the hat.

Let's connect the top of the hat.

Place the hat the part where you started knitting up: like this.

Insert the tail of the yarn inside every stitch on the left, from inside out.

Gently pull the tail after inserting in every stitch to connect the opening.

After inserting the tail into all 12 stitches, insert it into two of those that had the tail inserted before. *(This way the top will look beautiful!)*

Pull again to connect tightly.

Insert the tail into the center of the hat to hide it.

The top of your hat will look like a flower.

Turn the hat on the other side.

Weave in the tail.

Your hat is ready! Now we can attach a pom pom on the top or just wear it without one!

Here's how to add the pom pom:

Insert a needle with thread froom inside out.

Pom pom has a small hook in the middle: insert the needle with thread inside of it.

Then needle goes back inside the hat.

Repeat a few times until the pom pom is attached tightly.

Cut the thread.

Your beautiful hat with pom pom is ready!

Scarf with Pockets

Level: Intermediate

This cute scarf is made with Chunky chenille yarn. It has two pockets to make it very comfy.

Care: Wash in cold water on quick cycle, hang to dry or dry in a drying machine on medium heat.

What you will need:

- 2 skeins of Chunky Chenille yarn (we used Variegated color "Gray dream")
- Scissors

Cast on 5 stitches (Refer to pages 25-26).

Turn the chain over.

1st Row: Skip the first stitch.

We will be using the middle part of every stitch to pull out the first row.

Insert your hand inside that middle part of the stitch; grab working yarn and pull it out.

You just pulled out the second stitch in cast on row (first one we skipped).

Repeat pulling out stitches to the end of the row.

You now pulled out 5 stitches.

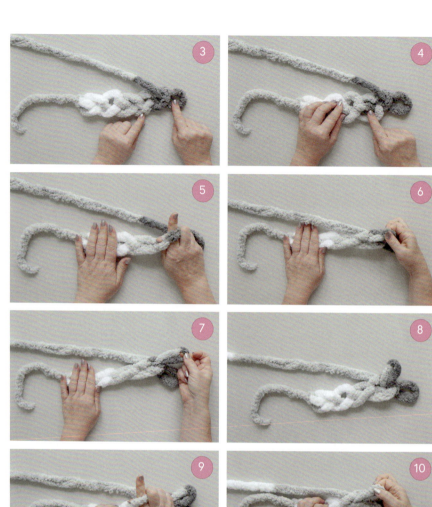

2nd Row: Insert your left hand inside the first stitch;

Grab working yarn.

Pull it out.

Repeat to all 5 stitches.

2nd row is done.

3rd Row: Starting this row we will skip knitting first stitch in every row to keep the ends of the scarf straight.

Insert your hand inside the second stitch;

Grab working yarn.

Pull it out.

Knit all 5 stitches.

Knit 6 rows total.

7th row: You will now purl all 5 stitches.

Place working yarn on the top of first stitch; push working yarn through the stitch.

Pull the stitch out.

Purl next 3 rows: 7-9.

Flip the scarf on another side and keep knitting for 65 rows: knitting is easier and faster than purling that is why we flipped the scarf on a side with knitting stitches.

The same as before when knitting, we will be skipping first stitch in every row and start knitting the second one.

When you knit all 65 rows, the scarf will look like this.

If you are out of yarn at this point — add another skein by making a simple knot.

Make it tight and then cut both tails of the knot close to the knot.

Now place both ends of the scarf in front of you like this: knitted parts beside each other and purled part on the left.

We will now purl all 5 stitches on the right part of the scarf to create the second pocket.

Purl 5 stitches.

Like this:

Keep purling for 6 rows.

Now let's **cast off** the last row on right side.

Take two first stitches, place them on your right hand.

Grab working yarn, pull it out.

You just knitted one stitch from two.

With your right hand inside last stitch, insert it inside the next stitch

Grab working yarn.

Pull it out to make one stitch from two.

When you cast off all stitches and have one left, cut the yarn to leave a tail about 10-12 inches.

Insert the tail inside the last stitch.

Pull it to finish the cast off of last row.

That is how the scarf will look like for now.

Place the scarf in front of you.

Fold first pocket as in the picture.

We will now connect two sides of each pocket to the scarf using that tail you left casting off:

Insert the tail inside the stitch on the back side of the scarf.

Then insert the tail inside the next stitch on the top side.

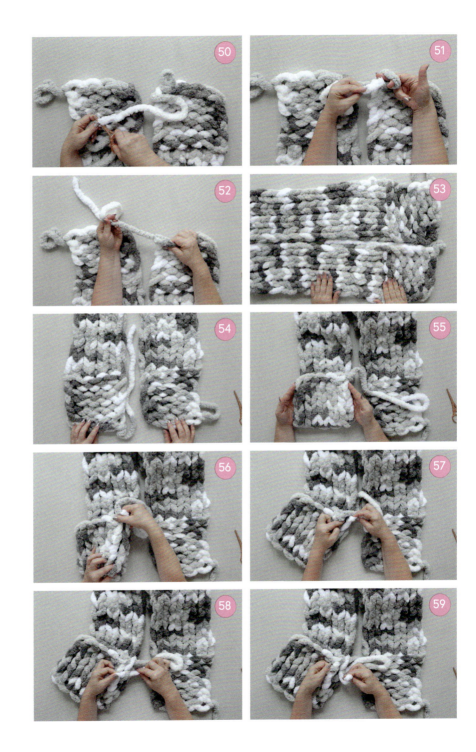

Keep inserting the tail in every stitch of the edge of the scarf: back and top.

Keep connecting the right side of the pocket this way.

When connected all stitches on this side: weave in the tail inside the pocket.

Cut a piece of yarn about 10-12 inches to connect the left side of the pocket.

Insert the tail inside two stitches on the bottom of the pocket: one from each side.

Now use the same technique as we used for the right side: insert the yarn in every stitch in both side, one by one.

Connect the tail to the back side of the scarf; weave in the tail.

Your pocket is done!

Now attach the second pocket the same way

Your Scarf with Pockets is finished!

Useful Techniques

Joining Super Chunky Merino Wool

When Hand knitting with Super chunky Merino wool, it needs to be connected in a special way: using a felting mat and needle.

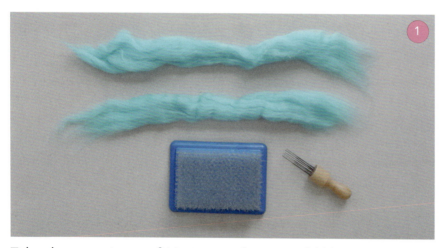

Take the two pieces of Merino wool you would like to join.

Thin out/fluff out the ends of each tail.

Place one tail on the felting mat.

Place the other tail on the top of it.

Take your felting needle and start to felt the two pieces together.

 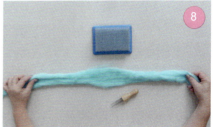

Now roll the connected spot.

Place in on the mat with the opening up.

Felt the opening to connect the ends together.

Make a Pom Pom

This pom pom is made with Super chunky Merino wool. It is fluffy and cute, perfect addition to a hat or a blanket.

What you need:

- 0.2 lbs of Super chunky Merino wool
- A string
- Sharp scissors

Place yarn on your left hand.

Wrap the wool around your four fingers loosely 6 times.

Take a string and place it under the wrapped yarn.

The string should be in the middle of the yarn.

Tie the string tight in the center of the wrapped yarn.

Make another knot to have it tight.

Hold the string in your hand.

Cut the wool loops on each end of the string.

The ends will look rough like this.

With both sides cut, fluff the pom pom with your hand.

Both sides.

Trim the pom pom to make it as round as possible.

The sharper the scissors — the better the result will be.

Your pom pom is finished and ready to go! Use the string to attach the pom pom to a hat or sides of your blanket.

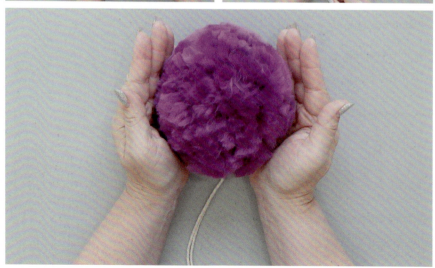

"BeCozi®" started as a home run hobby. Within the last 6 years it grew to a family business employing eight amazing people year-round and a few more — during Holidays. We call ourselves a 'BeCozi® family".

Thank you for all our supporters and followers.

BeCozi® is here because of all of YOU!